Eight. Seven. Six. Infinity

Arshiya Abuthahir

BookLeaf Publishing

Presentation by *BookLeaf Publishing*

Web: www.bookleafpub.com

E-mail: info@bookleafpub.com

ISBN: 9789357213509

First edition 2023

Hope

Hope
امل/Amal/Hope
/həʊp/

noun : a feeling of expectation and desire for a particular thing to happen.

Indeed there is hope in everything,
So, we must be calm and just hope.
Here's a hope that you achieve the purification of your soul,
Here's a hope that this life brings you blessings, joy and happiness that you prayed for,
Here's a hope that this life showers you with peace to your heart and home,
Here's a hope that this life brings you light all through your chaotic darkness,
Here's a hope that you successfully achieve all your aspirations,
Here's a hope that all your questions are answered,
Here's a hope that your life is filled with the Almighty's blessings and mercy,
Here's a hope that you infuse yourself with courage to Here's a hope face all the tests in life,

Here’s a hope that you get all that u desire for
Here’s a hope that this life gives you more
prosperity, faith, satisfaction and divine peace,
Here’s a hope that all your troubles are
burden-free,
Here’s a hope that the good times and the
beautiful,
present become treasurable memories of
tomorrow,
Here’s a hope to never lose hope, indeed here’s
hoping for a hope.

An Ode to Feriha

Begonia in here balcony,
A hot sip of coffee,
She startled to contemplate...
All the times, the minutes, the seconds.
She conspired to stand up on her feet,
For revolution.
The confusion she had,
Wanting to know the answers to her unanimous questions...
Her best friend Mija, a Persian kitten by her side,
Standing on a broken wooden pedestal,
There,
She was,
Terrible,
Angry,
It struck her chords,
She fell in love with a grey tinted corner in a way,
No one understood.
Feeling something was torn apart inside of her,
She drew a curve on her beautiful face,
Looking above the crows making a beautiful picture painted on the sky,

There she was with Mija, in her favourite darkest place.

Shipwreck Warrior

It might feel like almost all the time, I am isolated alone in the middle of an unnamed ocean,
I stand up on my deck and open the rugged map of life,
As the winds start to gaze, the map flies away and settles down the water as if it was meant to be there,
I don't know where I am going to head now,
My ship is filled with the dreams, the aspirations, the bright sun,
I now know that I cannot leave this behind and make all of me drown...
There are no stars up above there,
For me to route myself,
Life is making choices unheard, things unsaid.
How do I follow and head to where I belong?
I look around worried, anguish struck me,
That's what this journey is all about
There's something inside of me
I know, I know,
I can surpass the winds, the high tide waves,
I am all by myself,
Strong, A warrior,
I now know where I need to go,
Sailing through, I am coming home.

k • o • m • o • r • e • b • i

k • o • m • o • r • e • b • i

see the golden glare leaking through the leaves,
the way it's radiating, it's as if it's calling for
hope, calling all to be hopeful.
blink,
absorb,
smile,
breathe out,
feel the leaves through the eyes,
feel the word and the nature's beauty.
.
.
.
Komorebi
/ k ò m ó r é . b ì /
(n.) the way sun beams filter through the trees
and leaves of the forest.
木漏れ日
木 - tree, 漏れ - stem, 日 - day,Sun
ko. more. bi.

Rosé

A shade of you,
A shade of pink,
This colour I see,
The drops I feel,
Fallen down,
Hues of you,
Can I talk of the forest?

Verre ~ Glass

I dream to be happy, not broken or shattered into pieces.
I would miss my parts.
Something that worries me always is, fear of making a cut on you,
Wanting to give you out some melodic tunes but fearing to make you listen to my shattering pieces.
I want others to think of me as a living being, more than just a drinking glass, more than just a pudding inside of me, more than just a diamond, more than just a stand-up showpiece in a cupboard.
Sitting right there on the table to quench your thirst at night,
I sleep fine with my happy belly sometimes full, sometimes, sometimes half, sometimes empty, seeing my human makes me cozy and content.
I looked like a piece of art when I was being used for set out some delicious pineapple pudding instead of jar.
Layers on layers I looked perfectly and divine for you.

I kind of broke myself when I was at the edge of
the table, the thought that i could tell you I was
at the edge makes me feel guilty at times.
The point now in my life is to make you happy,
my siblings shiny, and not breaking myself into
small brittle pieces, not cutting your fingers.
I now stand like tall glass, slender work around
me with artistic touches,
I sit around looking at you and you looking at
me with warmth is all i need.
You treasure me.

You

cool.
happy.
generous.
slender.
beautiful.
these are just words which the society cultivates.
be yourself.
do anything and everything you love.
treat everyone with the same amount of respect.
and don't think anyone is as smaller than you.

Sunflower

how scorching the sun was,
that a flower withered amidst the cryptic and the chaos,
it’s time to bloom,
for real,
it’s time to blossom.

Baarish ~ Rain

sitting inside my car,
wondering to click a perfect shot,
but i couldn’t...
all i think is,
if people were rain and
the fact that they are happy to drizzle on me,
ruin my sunshine,
but sire...
turns out that i am a hurricane.

Dot it out, do it now

the world is getting smaller,
be open.
become tolerant.
accept.
listen.
advice.
repeat.
life is not a battle to be won.
put yourself in their shoes.
think. agree. disagree.
at last, you need to compromise.

Basics gets weirder

It all started from ABCs right,
and you thought it's going to be easy?
No,
It starts getting complicated.
You thought it was going to be smooth
But,
Didn't MNOP kind of broke it down?
I am sure,
You will make it to XYZ.

To my Fidan

This is for the woman in you Fidan,
You are a little princess, wearing the most enchanting gown and,
You have the most beautiful crown on your hair.
One day Fidan, you will grow,
That gown may or may not fit you but,
Your most beautiful crown would never get fat,
Fidan.

Mirror

you get to know your true self worth when you literally had a break up. it teaches you, to...
never.
ever.
shudder.
for less.

Life rules 101

it’s much better to get prepared,
mentally and physically,
to be alone.
because,
everyone is temporary.
their shitty mouth is theirs,
don’t bother considering their shit.

there...

there will be ups
there will be downs
there will be sadness
there will be grief
but there is no ‘giving up’
you might think that is easy to tell all this rather
than practicing in real life.
there is your life, happy and beautiful.

blue

sea will be rough.
waves will be higher.
stay there.
try for hours.
and then,
breath of fresh air.

Accept ~ stance

acceptance.
acceptance is what this whole circle of life has taught me.
and I am sure it has taught all of us by now,
most importantly, it has taught me the acceptance of myself.

Done.

i won't do it.
i can't do it.
i want to do it.
how do i do it.
i'll try to do it.
i can do it.
i will do it.
yes i did it.

Per, you

make sometime for yourself.
you are busy?
priorities yourself.
gift your self,
pamper,
hamper,
but don’t tamper.

Just you

appreciate how special you are,
no one is like us, you have your special talent.
share it with the universe.
everyone might have the same as yours,
but how you use it, is different,
because you are unique.
you created your own unique reality.
you are a big shot.

Pro tip

shamelessly,
love yourself.

www.ingramcontent.com/pod-product-compliance
Lightning Source LLC
Chambersburg PA
CBHW051719130826
49812CB00034B/1262
* 9 7 8 9 3 5 7 2 1 3 5 0 9 *